31.35

796.332

D1361604

# 12 REASONS TO LOVE
# FOOTBALL

by Brian Howell

12 STORY LIBRARY

www.12StoryLibrary.com

12-Story Library is an imprint of Bookstaves and Press Room Editions.

Produced for 12-Story Library by Red Line Editorial

Photographs ©: Jack Dempsey/AP Images, cover, 1; dean bertoncelj/Shutterstock Images, 4; Jun Ji/Shutterstock Images, 5; Tony Tomsic/AP Images, 6; Joseph Sohm/Shutterstock Images, 7, 14; Dave Martin/AP Images, 8, 29; Nick Wass/AP Images, 9; Jim Mahoney/ AP Images, 10; Africa Studio/Shutterstock Images, 11; Jeremy R. Smith Sr./Shutterstock Images, 12; David Durochik/AP Images, 13; Katherine Welles/Shutterstock Images, 15; Nick Lisi/AP Images, 16, 28; Al Messerschmidt/AP Images, 17; Pictorial News Co/Library of Congress, 18; Mark Herreid/Shutterstock Images, 19; Scott Boehm/AP Images, 20; Tom Hauck/AP Images, 21; John Gaps III/AP Images, 22; AP Images, 23; Aspen Photo/ Shutterstock Images, 24; Helga Esteb/Shutterstock Images, 25; Albert Cesare/Opelika- Auburn News/AP Images, 27

**Library of Congress Cataloging-in-Publication Data**
A catalog record for this book is available from the Library of Congress
978-1-63235-427-3 (hardcover)
978-1-63235-496-9 (paperback)
978-1-62143-548-8 (ebook)

Printed in China
022017

# Table of Contents

# Football Is America's Game

In the United States, fans love a wide variety of sports. Americans love to watch baseball, basketball, soccer, hockey, and golf. But nothing draws fans like football.

The National Football League (NFL) is the most popular sports league in the United States. The NFL features 32 teams in 22 states. The teams are divided into two conferences: the American Football Conference (AFC) and the National Football Conference (NFC).

Millions of fans watch every NFL game. The NFL season begins in September and ends in early January. It's followed by the playoffs and Super Bowl. Approximately a third of US sports fans say NFL football is their favorite. The NFL is even more popular than baseball, which has long been considered "the national pastime."

The Dallas Cowboys are one of the NFL's most popular teams.

# $2.34 billion

**Average worth of an NFL team in 2016.**

- Sports fans love NFL football more than any other sport.
- There are 32 teams in the NFL.
- College football is also very popular.

Fans also have a passion for college football. College teams play at schools in small towns and big cities across the country. In 2016, there were 774 college football teams. It was a record number.

## INTERNATIONAL FOOTBALL

The NFL has been working to grow the game outside the United States. Between 1991 and 2007, the NFL oversaw a league in Europe. It went by several names, including the World League of American Football and NFL Europa. It was a feeder league, which means the players were NFL prospects. Since 2007, the NFL has played at least one game per year in London, England.

College football is so big that 10 percent of US sports fans call it their favorite sport.

Michigan Stadium can seat more than 107,000 Wolverines fans.

# 2

# The NFL Has Legendary Players

Some of the greatest athletes in sports history have played football. Some of those athletes were so great they became legends.

Jim Brown is one of the most legendary players in football history. Brown played for the Cleveland Browns from 1957 to 1965. He was one of the greatest running backs ever. In only nine seasons, he rushed for 12,312 career yards. It was a record for many years. Brown is a legend off the field as well. He has acted in movies and mentored young people.

New England Patriots quarterback Tom Brady is a legend, too. Brady came into the NFL in 2000. He was never expected to be a star.

In 2001, the Patriots' starting quarterback, Drew Bledsoe, was injured. Brady took over and has been a superstar ever since. He led the Patriots to three Super Bowl victories in his first four years as

Jim Brown was the first player ever to run more than 10,000 career yards.

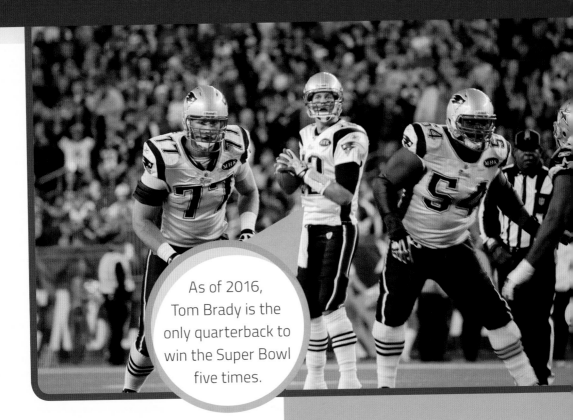

As of 2016, Tom Brady is the only quarterback to win the Super Bowl five times.

a starter. He won his fifth Super Bowl after the 2016 season. He's known as one of the best players in football history.

# 1984

**Year Walter Payton broke Jim Brown's career rushing record.**

- Some of the best athletes have played in the NFL.
- Jim Brown was a legend on and off the field.
- Tom Brady wasn't expected to be a star but became one of the best NFL quarterbacks ever.

## THE HALL OF FAME

Football's greatest players and coaches end up in the Pro Football Hall of Fame. Located in Canton, Ohio, the hall displays busts of the more than 300 members inducted. To be eligible, a person must have not played or coached in the previous five seasons. Each year the hall holds an induction ceremony, where new members give speeches.

# Fans Love Their Team Heroes

Football fans love their hometown NFL teams. The players on those teams often become local heroes.

John Elway grew up in California. But once he joined the Broncos in 1983, he became the heart of Denver. During his career from 1983 to 1998, Elway led the Broncos to five Super Bowls. They lost three of them. But in his final two seasons, he spurred the Broncos to back-to-back Super Bowl

John Elway celebrates his first Super Bowl.

championships. He now acts as general manager for the team.

Linebacker Ray Lewis became a hero to the people of Baltimore. Lewis played for the Ravens from 1996 to 2012. The city loved his passion and how hard he played the game. One of the best linebackers in history, he was a great leader for the team, too. Lewis led the Ravens to two Super Bowl wins. He's considered one of the best defensive players in league history.

Quarterback Russell Wilson has become a local hero in Seattle. Drafted by the Seahawks in 2012, he was expected to be their backup. Instead, he won the starting job as a rookie. The team and fans love his athletic ability and his leadership. In

# 2000
**Year Ray Lewis was named Super Bowl MVP.**

- Great players become heroes in their communities.
- John Elway was the heart of the Denver Broncos.
- Russell Wilson led Seattle to two Super Bowls.
- Ray Lewis was a team leader for the Ravens.

2013, Wilson led the Seahawks to their first championship. He helped the team reach another Super Bowl the very next year, though they lost. He's the first quarterback to play in two Super Bowls in his first three seasons.

Ray Lewis pumps up fans with his signature dance.

# Super Bowl Sunday Is the Best

The one event sports fans can't miss is the Super Bowl. Every year, more Americans watch the Super Bowl than any other TV show. Nearly 112 million people watched Super Bowl 50 in 2016.

Fans tune in because the game features the two best teams in the league. The winner will be named NFL champion. Some Super Bowls are considered the best games in football history. Fans voted the Patriots-Seahawks Super Bowl in

Super Bowl Sunday is a spectacular event.

Football-themed snacks are often found at Super Bowl parties.

huge audience. New, creative commercials are shown throughout the game. A 30-second ad cost $5 million to air during the Super Bowl in February 2016.

February 2015 as the greatest game of all time.

People watch the Super Bowl for more than just the game action, however. The pregame and halftime shows are also entertaining. In fact, the halftime show is like a miniconcert.

Many people watch only for the commercials. With more than 100 million viewers, it's a great chance for advertisers to reach a

Around the United States, people hold Super Bowl parties every year, even if their favorite team isn't playing. They gather with friends and family to watch the game and commercials. And, of course, eat lots of food.

## $82.19
**Estimated average amount each viewer spent on food, party supplies, and merchandise for Super Bowl Sunday in 2016.**

- The Super Bowl is the most watched show on US television each year.
- The Super Bowl features the two best NFL teams.
- Many people tune in to watch the halftime show and commercials.

## THINK ABOUT IT

Compare the commercials shown during the Super Bowl to those shown during a news show. What differences do you notice? What do the commercials tell you about the people watching the Super Bowl?

11

# College Football Rules Saturdays

The NFL captures sports fans' attention every Sunday throughout the fall. Saturdays, however, belong to college football.

The highest level of college football is Division I of the National Collegiate Athletic Association (NCAA). There are more than 125 Division I football teams. Some of the most notable teams include

## THINK ABOUT IT

The top college football programs generate millions of dollars. But college football players don't make any money. Some, but not all, players simply get to attend college for free. Some people believe college players should be paid. Do you agree? Why or why not?

The cheer squad leads the Notre Dame team onto the field.

# 1935

**Year Jay Berwanger of the University of Chicago won the first Heisman Trophy.**

- The best college football teams play in Division I of the NCAA.
- The Heisman Trophy is awarded each year to the best college player.
- College football fans are enthusiastic about their teams.

Ohio State were tied for the most Heisman winners. They had seven Heisman winners each. The only player to win the Heisman twice is Ohio State's Archie Griffin.

College football games are fun to attend. There are marching bands, rowdy students, and great traditions. College football fans can be even more passionate about their teams than NFL fans.

the University of Notre Dame, the University of Alabama, and Ohio State University.

Division I teams battle each week to be ranked among the Top 25. At the end of the year, the best four teams compete in a playoff. The winner of that playoff is crowned the national champion.

Each year, the Heisman Trophy is awarded to the top player in college football. Through the 2015 season, Notre Dame and

Archie Griffin won the Heisman in 1974 and 1975.

# 6

# Friday Night Lights Shine Bright

Before players become stars in the NFL, they make their mark in high school. Many high schools play their games under the bright lights on Friday nights in the fall.

In 2016, more than 1.1 million high school students played football for their schools. Traditionally, football games feature 11 players per team on the field. Some leagues require as few as six players on the field per team. More high school students play football than any other sport. Of the 1.1 million students playing football in 2016, nearly 2,000 were girls. The number of girls playing football has seen its ups and downs over the years. Since 2008, it's been on the rise.

High school football is great because of its fans. In many towns across the country, the local high school football game is

Across the country, high school football brings people together.

a major event. The entire community shows up to root for the team. Playing under the Friday night lights, the players are the pride of their hometowns.

In some areas, high school football is as big as college or even NFL football. In Texas, high school football is king. The best teams in the state sometimes play in NFL stadiums. In Las Vegas, Nevada, Bishop Gorman High School is a football powerhouse. A private school, Gorman has training facilities that are better than some colleges' facilities.

## 54,347
**Number of fans who watched Allen High School take on Pearland High School in 2013, setting the all-time attendance record for Texas high school football.**

- More high school students play football than any other sport.
- Nearly 2,000 girls played football in 2016.
- Some high school programs draw huge crowds and have top-of-the-line facilities.

AT&T Stadium, home of the Dallas Cowboys, hosts some Texas high school games.

# Some Plays Are Unforgettable

University of Louisville quarterback Lamar Jackson tucked the ball into his left arm and took off running. Near the 7-yard line, a defender from Syracuse University lowered his shoulder and tried to make the tackle. But he never even touched Jackson.

Jackson leaped high in the air and jumped right over the defender. He ran to the end zone for a touchdown.

Amazing plays such as Jackson's make football easy to love. Great plays happen at the NFL, college, and youth football levels. When players are loaded with talent and athletic ability, the unexpected can happen at any time. For instance, in 2007, San Diego's Antonio Cromartie returned a missed field goal 109 yards for a touchdown. That's the longest touchdown distance possible. In 2013, Minnesota's Cordarrelle Patterson also had a 109-yard kickoff return for a touchdown.

Lamar Jackson leaps for his amazing touchdown.

The Music City Miracle kept the Titans in the playoffs, and they eventually reached the Super Bowl.

One of the most amazing plays took place on January 8, 2000. The Buffalo Bills had a 16–15 lead over the Tennessee Titans. There were 16 seconds left. Buffalo kicked the ball off to Tennessee. The Titans needed a miracle. Lorenzo Neal caught the kickoff. He handed it off to Frank Wycheck. Next, Wycheck threw it across the field to teammate Kevin Dyson. From there, Dyson sprinted 75 yards for the game-winning touchdown. Tennessee won 22–16. The play is known as the Music City Miracle.

## 32

**Number of yards gained on the Helmet Catch by David Tyree to set up a Giants victory in Super Bowl 42.**

- Amazing plays make fans love football.
- Lamar Jackson leaped over a defender in a game for Louisville.
- The Music City Miracle won a game for the Tennessee Titans.

# Old and New Stadiums Are Impressive

Football fans are known to travel to games just to see a certain stadium. Some of the famous stadiums are old while others are new.

In the NFL, few stadiums have more history than Lambeau Field in Green Bay, Wisconsin. Home to the Packers, Lambeau opened in 1957. Some of the greatest games in NFL history have taken place there.

And some of the most famous players made Lambeau their home. College football features many historic stadiums as well. The University of Pennsylvania has played at Franklin Field since 1895. Harvard Stadium opened in 1903.

But not all stadiums are impressive because they're historic. Some of the most amazing stadiums are brand new and state of the art. The San Francisco 49ers opened Levi's

Some of the first football games in history were played at Harvard Stadium.

## STADIUM SUCCESS

Some college stadiums have seen decades of success. Notre Dame Stadium has been home to the Fighting Irish since 1930. Over the years, seven Heisman Trophy winners have played there, and the school has won nine national championships.

# $1.5 billion

**Cost of Mercedes-Benz Stadium, home of the Atlanta Falcons.**

- Football stadiums draw in fans.
- Lambeau Field is a historic NFL stadium.
- New stadiums have state-of-the-art features.

Stadium in 2014. Fans can use a special app on their smartphones to order food and watch replays. In 2016, the Minnesota Vikings opened US Bank Stadium. It boasts the world's largest working doors to create an open-air feel. The Atlanta Falcons opened Mercedes-Benz Stadium in 2017. Its retractable roof can open and close in only seven minutes. Another huge stadium is currently under construction. When the Rams agreed to move to Los Angeles, construction began on their new home, City of Champions Stadium.

US Bank Stadium is the home of the Minnesota Vikings.

# Football Has Favorite Traditions

Football is full of beloved traditions. Fans look forward to these special moments every year or even at every game. This is true for the NFL and for every other level of the sport.

In college football, few traditions are as exciting as the way the University of Colorado Buffaloes start each home game. Ralphie—a live buffalo weighing 1,200 pounds—leads the team onto the field. Another great tradition can be found at Ohio State. The marching band forms the word *Ohio* at every home game. Sometimes a celebrity or important person gets the honor of being the dot for the letter *i*.

Some of the best traditions in football are

Ralphie charges onto the field with the help of several handlers.

Davante Adams does the Lambeau Leap after a touchdown.

the rivalries between teams. Since 1916, Harvard University and Yale University have faced off against each other in football. Fans of both teams look forward to the heated rivalry each year.

In the NFL, one great tradition happens on a holiday. Each year since 1934, the Detroit Lions have played on Thanksgiving. Other teams have played many times on Thanksgiving as well, including the Dallas Cowboys.

Another fun NFL tradition brings fans and players closer together—literally. After many touchdowns at home games, Green Bay Packers players jump into the stands to celebrate with fans. It's known as the Lambeau Leap. It began in 1993.

# 1875

**Year the rivalry between Norwich Free Academy and New London began, making it the oldest rivalry in high school football.**

- Football fans look forward to the special traditions of the sport.
- In college football, one tradition is the Ohio State marching band forming the word *Ohio*.
- The Detroit Lions have played on every Thanksgiving since 1934.

# Great Tackles Have Won Games

Many football games have been won by last-second touchdowns. But sometimes stopping a touchdown can win a game in the final moments. A great tackle can save a team.

In 2000, the Super Bowl came down to the final play. The Tennessee Titans had one last chance to score a touchdown. Steve McNair passed to Kevin Dyson. Dyson sprinted toward the end zone. But Mike Jones of the St. Louis Rams got a hand on Dyson's leg. Dyson stretched as far as he could. But Jones brought him down him at the 1-yard line. The tackle won the Super Bowl for the Rams.

Sometimes the whole defense can make a big stop. In the 1979 Sugar Bowl, Alabama led Penn State 14–7 in the fourth quarter. The winner

Kevin Dyson reaches for the end zone, but Mike Jones stops him.

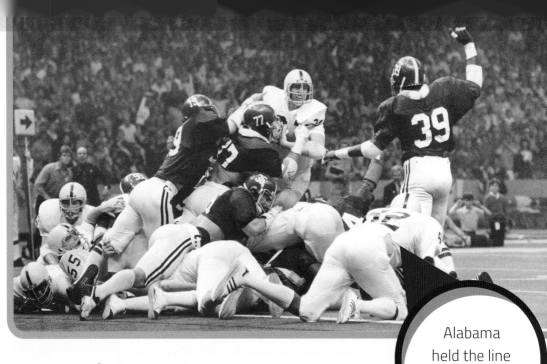

Alabama held the line in the 1979 Sugar Bowl.

would be the national champion. Penn State had the ball at Alabama's 1-yard line. But the Alabama defense held firm. They stopped Penn State on two straight plays. Thanks to that goal-line stand, Alabama held on to win the game.

## 25

**Record number of tackles by Brian Urlacher of the Chicago Bears in a 2006 game against the Arizona Cardinals.**

- Great tackles can mean the difference between winning and losing.
- A tackle at the 1-yard line saved the Super Bowl for the St. Louis Rams.
- Alabama defeated Penn State on a goal-line stand in the 1979 Sugar Bowl.

## AN UNUSUAL TACKLER

In 2015, Connecticut high school player Hudson Hamill was running upfield when he was suddenly hit hard. It caused a fumble. It was a great tackle—except it was made by the referee. While just an accident, the fumble counted. Thankfully, Hamill's team still went on to win.

23

# Players Have Speed to Burn

The NFL wows fans with some of the fastest players ever to play the sport. Wide receivers catch the ball. They rely on their speed to get open for the catch and to keep running for the end zone. Willie Gault and Randy Moss are two of the speediest receivers in NFL history. Gault even won a bronze medal for hurdles at the 1983 World Championships.

However, two of the fastest NFL stars were cornerbacks. Cornerbacks defend against wide receivers. Hall of Famers Deion Sanders and Darrell Green were two of the fastest cornerbacks. Sanders was a flashy player known as Prime Time. Green was widely regarded as the NFL's fastest player in the late 1980s.

Football is a game of speed, and some players have plenty of it.

## THE COMBINE

Many NFL hopefuls take part in the NFL Scouting Combine each year. The combine lets teams evaluate players through a number of events. One of the most-watched tests is the 40-yard dash. As of 2016, Chris Johnson holds the record for fastest time.

# 10.6

**Seconds in which Dallas Cowboys star "Bullet" Bob Hayes ran the 100-meter dash to win gold at the 1964 Olympics.**

- Some of the fastest players are wide receivers such as Willie Gault.
- Deion Sanders and Darrell Green were fast cornerbacks.
- Running backs such as Chris Johnson are known for their sprints.

Chris Johnson ran a 40-yard dash in 4.24 seconds at the NFL combine.

Of course, running backs must be fast, too. Running back Chris Johnson was one of the fastest players ever. He was a star with the Tennessee Titans. Johnson regularly outran defenses with his deadly speed. Between 2009 and 2012, he had six touchdown runs of 80 yards or longer. Once he got into the open, nobody could catch him.

# Fantastic Finishes Amaze Fans

On any given game day, something spectacular could happen on the football field. For instance, many amazing things happen when the game is on the line.

During the 2013 season, Auburn University trailed the University of Georgia by one point. There were only 25 seconds left. Auburn was 73 yards away from the end zone. Auburn quarterback Nick Marshall

threw the ball downfield. The ball bounced off a Georgia defender. It floated in the air. For a moment, Auburn receiver Ricardo Louis couldn't see the ball. Then it fell right into his arms. He took it in for the game-winning touchdown.

## 38
**Consecutive points Michigan State scored— including a field goal in the final seconds—to beat Northwestern 41–38 in 2006.**

- Football games often come down to thrilling last-second plays.
- Auburn beat Georgia with an unbelievable touchdown catch in the final seconds.
- On the last play before overtime, DeSean Jackson scored on a game-winning punt return.

## THINK ABOUT IT

Imagine you're a football player. There are only seconds left in the game. The right play could win you the game—and the wrong play could lose it. Design a play that might win the game. Why do you think your play will work? What play would you not run?

In 2010, one the most miraculous NFL finishes occurred. The New York Giants led the Philadelphia Eagles 31–10 with less than eight minutes to play. But then the Eagles managed to score 21 straight points to tie the game. The game seemed headed for overtime. On the last play, the Giants punted. Philadelphia's DeSean Jackson returned the kick 65 yards for the game-winning touchdown.

Ricardo Louis scores the game-winning touchdown for Auburn.

# Fact Sheet

- On September 10, 2016, the University of Tennessee and Virginia Tech University played at Bristol Motor Speedway in Tennessee. Nearly 157,000 fans attended the game. It was the largest crowd ever for an American football game.

- The Green Bay Packers and the Chicago Bears have the NFL's oldest rivalry. Their first meeting was in 1921, when the Bears were known as the Chicago Staleys. Chicago won 20–0.

- During his career from 1998 to 2015, Peyton Manning directed 45 fourth-quarter comeback victories—the most of any quarterback.

- In 2009, just 35 seconds remained on the clock when the Pittsburgh Steelers' Santonio Holmes caught a touchdown pass to beat the Arizona Cardinals in the Super Bowl. Earlier in the game, Pittsburgh linebacker James Harrison set a Super Bowl record when he returned an interception 100 yards for a touchdown.

- The Rose Bowl is known as the Granddaddy of Them All. It's the oldest bowl game by far. The first Rose Bowl was played in Pasadena, California, in 1902.

- Jerry Rice is regarded as the greatest wide receiver of all time. The former San Francisco 49ers star holds the NFL career records for most receptions, receiving yards, and touchdown catches.

# Glossary

**consecutive**
Following one after another in a series.

**draft**
When an athlete is chosen to play for a team.

**induction**
The formal act of making someone a member.

**league**
A collection of teams that compete against one another.

**legend**
A person who is very famous for his or her achievements.

**mentor**
Someone who teaches or guides younger people.

**powerhouse**
A person or team that is very skilled.

**retractable**
Able to be pulled back.

**rivalry**
A fierce and ongoing competition between two or more teams.

**tradition**
A pattern or set way of doing something over time.

# For More Information

## Books

*Big Book of Who: Football.* New York: Time Home Entertainment Inc., 2013.

Gitlin, Marty. *Cam Newton: Football Star.* Lake Elmo, MN: Focus Readers, 2017.

Kelley, K. C. *Football Superstars 2015.* New York: Scholastic Inc., 2015.

## Visit 12StoryLibrary.com

Scan the code or use your school's login at **12StoryLibrary.com** for recent updates about this topic and a full digital version of this book. Enjoy free access to:

- Digital ebook
- Breaking news updates
- Live content feeds
- Videos, interactive maps, and graphics
- Additional web resources

**Note to educators:** Visit 12StoryLibrary.com/register to sign up for free premium website access. Enjoy live content plus a full digital version of every 12-Story Library book you own for every student at your school.

# Index

## About the Author

Brian Howell has been a sports journalist for more than 20 years. He has written dozens of books about sports. A native of Colorado, he lives in Denver with his wife and children.